Glass Houses and Stone

Poetry

By

Alison C. Seaton

Eternal Water Publications books may be ordered through Amazon.com or at: www.eternalwaterpublications.com

Eternal Water Publications LLC.
P.O. Box 880373 Port St. Lucie Florida, 34988

The views expressed in this work are solely those of the author and do not necessarily reflect the views of the publisher, and the publisher hereby disclaims any responsibility for them.

Any people depicted in stock imagery provided by Istockphoto are models, and such images are being used for illustrative purposes only.

Cover image is provided by ©Istockphoto

Embedded photos taken by the author

ISBN: 978-0-9968971-2-9

Printed in the United States of America

Eternal Water Publications

TABLE OF CONTENTS

Dedication

To my Father and Mother,

Who encouraged me over the years and created in me an appreciation for the discipline and the art of writing. I have been inspired by your written work.

To my High School English Teacher-Mr. Brand wherever you are:

Thank you for your inspiration and for taking my curiosity, dreams, drive, light and dark moments, and showing me how to give them life on paper.

Glass Houses and Stone

Section 1 - **Love Poems**

The Night is Long

Indeed, the night is long and trees are scarce.
I look around to see your face
yet instead, there's miles and miles of barren sea
bathed in blue silver, facing greenery.
And still puzzled the breakers crash
hoping for solace with every thrash.
Miles and miles of barren sea
Ache to summon your vision to me.

The birds will sing but not at night.
It is the cricket and cicadas right
to hold sway over a wandering soul,
bereft of sleep and lover's hold.
I'd rather feel green and gravel 'neath my feet
than be cushioned without you, my sweet.
And so this wandering soul does walk this way,
gladly being held in sway.

So stationary on this spinning globe
Is marching time that enrobes
All who search for love and loved ones lent
To Country, to Duty, to sacrifice!
It is ethereal this thing called hope –
Yet possess it we must to regain
our soul's breath, yes! Our heart's eye

so hope ethereal be personified
in us for now, and for all time.

Intolerable night taking lesson from the trees,
Yields my lover's smile on its knees.
Until next time silver sea, gravel and green,
gentle sleep; entangle me with my love's feet.

Finally

Finally! I said when I first saw his face
A man with whom I can really dance.
The timber of his voice, the firmness of his touch
the hush of awareness echoed in his eyes.
And I began to be afraid.

He is not a man of many words
but what he says is measured well.
He is not a man of flighty tongue
but when his lips brush- ooh indelible colors.
And exult I begin to, Indeed.

To be touched by him is no superficial thrill
The trembling starts from deep within.
To be held by him means no escape...
and still the trembling will not leave-
Its solid communion with skin on skin.

Is it he? My soul asks yearningly
Or just the magic of light, laughter and chemistry?
Is it truly meant to be?
Or just the caprice of time,
place, and handsome face?

It's already too late to draw back now.
The gong's been beaten into the ground.
One flattering smile – fluttering lid
Has just simply done me in.
And so, afraid and happy I stand
hoping the pleasure will be worth the pain.

Dance

May I have this dance?
Dance! With you?
Yes, dance the Dance of Life with me.
Waltz, sashay, and pirouette.

Will you give me your heart?
My heart! Why?
Why, because I have need of it.
Please comply, don't be shy.

Give me your soul.
My being, my very being?
You must be mad!
No just crazy for you
and I know you'll feel so too
If you'll let go.

In return
Take my breath, blood, sinew and bones.
Let my arms encase you as skin.
Feel me, Flow into me, Be one.

How was I supposed to know?

When you sadly tried to end it
I felt my blood freeze
We'd never really even begun to soar…
I'd dreamed of this the night before.

The tears of my dream refused to well up now
But the urgency to keep you was there.
I said everything I could to change your mind
And lo, you have come back to me…
Perhaps you never meant to leave at all
But, how was I to know?

On a Starry Night

On a starry night
When you behold the lights
Think of me awhile
And breathe a prayer

For on yon little starry
I also would tarry
And lisp a psalm
With you in mind.

Betwixt us both
Yet not at all –
Same star will see us
Together again.

Pipedream

From we met
I believed
That it would be nice
If we could get together…

Not only nice, but
magical
But now I see
That we weren't meant to be….

Yes, now I realize
that I was just chasing a pipe dream
again….

Seems Like Forever

Though it seems like forever
I will wait for you.
Though it reeks of never
I'll always search for you.
Perhaps obsessed is the best word
Or, besotted maybe…

I only know you hold all of me,
Every nerve, breath, move; each sigh.
In everything you are there.
I sleep and you ride the crests of my dreams.
I work and store up things to tell you.
When closing my eyes for an instant your face swims close.
Your voice soothes me.

It is utterly impossible to feel like this I tell myself.
Yet impracticality confuses fact.
What do I know of you except that you feel right-
After I've been with you, I can't erase your imprint.
So…
If this is infatuation and love is the next stage
I don't want to fall in love.

Roses, Just Because

Impatient! That's what I am at living
Rushing into relationships heady with plans for giving.
I long for morning embraces with Mr. Right
And am not thinking of problems that may come to light-
Just a baby, a home, a husband, a mate.

Self deprivation is a thing of my past
So I fly headlong, seeking, into relationships, hoping they'll last.
I long for pitter-pat feet and that deep male voice at the door-
Daddy's home, called out, while I go about my chores.

I long for Roses at Mother's day, birthdays, and just because-
The Fortunoff Anniversary bracelet, solitaire, or a pretty vase.
Retiring together, grey hair together, together after all those years
And the kids coming to visit, bringing their fiancées.

I long for all of this and Roses just because…
Yes. Just because: for Roses.

Kisses

Our love was born from the wailing surrender
of passion pushing painfully 'tween knees of sacrifice.
And I love you. I love you innocently, purely, totally.
Where do I end and you begin? In our kisses!

Embraces prolong pleasure poignantly sweet; mélange to panacea;
As your hand touches, all nerves register
pressure, release, cold hot, soft hard, bleeding then healing
and all I want is for it to never end. Then more kisses.

Laugh quarrel speak refrain, thrust parry,
the heart has its own rhythm,
Want you, need you, love you, kiss you, want you, need you, love
you…
Drown me in chaste or deep kisses. Then even more kisses.

Isn't that Love?

Ever let a man love you?
I mean love you
Without saying a word
Just eyes on eyes, lips on lips
Skin on skin and rhythm to rhythm
Was it love?

Ever let a man touch you?
I mean really touch you
with thoughtful gestures
At just the right time
Tokens, kisses, hugs, notes, lick away your tears.
Was it love?

Ever let a man reach you
I mean really reach you
That kernel deep inside
Blossom at the thought, sight, smell and taste of him
Was it love?

I say women, how about a man loving you?
I mean the eternal, for life, loving you-
Talk with you, relate to you, mate for life,
kids with you kind of loving you.
Now, isn't that love?

Blackbird

I felt a oneness with the Blackbird in the tree
A mirror of the melancholy that was me.
Perched amidst the blossoms meant to be –
fruit or flowers?
Attracting insects and an early season Bumblebee

This is the hour of malaise that catches me
When midstream I contemplate a new direction,
new task, a new love.
The torrential stream catches my driftwood and swirling all about,
bears me up like an offering.
Roiling me along, molding, refining, redefining, polishing, honing,
creating, a new me.

The winds gently toss the molting branches on which I perch.
What change does their whisper bring – I search.
I search the fronds for discernment
But fear of fulfillment, or it withheld, holds me aloft
to ponder some more.
The Blackbird and I tilt our heads – listing, waiting
with a keening feeling, for the hidden message.

I felt a oneness with the Blackbird in the tree.
A trilling call roused the melancholy from deep within me.
And it was gone.
Behind was left a rustling and....
The bothersome hum of this season's early Bumblebee

Gifts

My lover's gift's are –
Honey Brown Eyes
Molten Molasses running down
Deep inside me and all around

Smiles, wide, slow
Light beams and rainbows
Reflecting hearts – then
Mischievous glows.

Silk, satin, flutters
Draw taught my bow
The melody rings Constancy Now!

A bower of protection is
The certainty of trust
coupled with respect –
Forging a pledge no one can oust.

Love's Prayer

I asked the Lord for a mate if it be His will
And His answer in You, has me in awe and reverence still.
We were walking through time to this pivotal point
Guided by God, his servant's sincerest desires don't disappoint.

May our prayers to Him, a constant incense be,
And His light and love in us be to all a canopy –
That warms each one we meet,
And drives them to worship at His feet.

Dear God, let us grow old together gracefully,
Hone our love into an eternal fire for all to see.
Your will, enshrine upon our hearts
And make us one, forever! Never to part.

Only You

I'm worried about my state of mind
Desperation for a partner has me tunnel blind
 for You, only You.

You're not haughty or from any elite
A lawyer or doctor, even engineer, but my heart beats
for You, only You.

Sleep I chase yet cannot catch
Food is eaten only with survivor's dispatch
because of You, only You.

I curse my weakness each time I call
Why the hell for you did I fall
yes for You, only You?

Kiss me, let's make up once more
I promise, I'll never show you the door
Want You, only You.

Love's Legacy

Love revisited is return to a favorite season
An event from which the heart beats out rhyme without reason.

One sets out to walk defining the feet's destination
Yet, yields to the path plod by the heart's pedantic ultimatum

I tried to determine the constraints my heart should espouse
And found that memory of one word, look, one touch, still would
arouse.

Construction of boundaries, a task so fain –
Leads me through temporary triumphant plains – such bittersweet
gains.

Alas, the revolution brings irrefutable end
to love, marked so on my heart – A legend!

I no longer set the course but let the rudder run free
Perhaps in time a new love will yield more promising legacy.

Brown Eyes, Why?

How do you propose to hold my heart
When another has shredded it all apart?
Your Brown Eyes have church awe worship,
burning deep to my hidden place.
I'm not ready to run again at this hectic pace.
Drowning, suffocating, as I rise from this Chrysalis –
And you are still here Brown Eyes. Why?

How do you purport to match my fire?
The banked embers, evidence of negligence at stoking.
Your brown arms around me have turned the chill
into this warming, glowing, thing.
I'm not ready for sparks that fly and singe at will.
Glowing, gleaming, shining, I flicker forth
And you are still here Brown Eyes. Why?

What tale of love do you endeavor to write?
Prior pages and pens have ripped or exploded –
Dripping their dark dank ink on my door
The angel of mercy has always ignored me before.
Your kisses taste like passion with patience
An essence I have never tasted 'fore now
Brown Eyes, you're still here. Why?

When you propose to write this new script
you'd better be damn sure you are equipped
for my foibles, upswings, the tenement and ghetto places we may
reach.
And most of all the nakedness, intimate nakedness
Brown Eyes you're still here facing my fire
You are still here despite my defense
Brown Eyes, you're still here. Still here, why?

(inspired by Sting's – 'Be Still my beating heart' amongst other
things….)

Elements of Love

Where there is love, the hearts of two
Cleave into one and a shared vision is formed.
Where there is love, a man will sacrifice for,
And honor the woman he chooses to bring home.
Where there is love, each one gifts the other
Just to see a smile or sparkle in the eye.
Where there is love, each one' s heart
beats faster on sight – souls together fly.

Where there is love, the woman supports,
Inspires, challenges, and defends her man.
Where there is love, conflicts and anger fleet
Across pages where forgiveness and patience have greater voice.

Where there is love, each one learns to bring out
the best in the other and forge the worst into better over time.
Where there is love, honesty seeps under every door-
Integrity beckons others who look on.
People say – You are so in love,
How did you keep the romance going after all those years?
The reply – There was always love.

Glass and Stone

I speak - my love story, unique,
There is only one passion, despite countless lifelines.
Cleaved from cliffs made eons ago
and uplifted on bubbling fires,
I stood lonely and resolute.

What is it like to be ravaged by the passing years,
the elements, man who marks for pleasure or profit
and still be standing, but alone? So alone!
Darkened by wind tossed rain, bleached by Lichen emissions and
sun
Chiseled to reveal my beauty by the Master's,
I am proud nevertheless, for the pain, never the less.

My lover was born from lightening on distant shores
then man molded in fires red, blue, white, hot
It was then her beauty was seen in all its forms
and I was smitten, when for me smiting was the norm.
I was lonely no more.

I courted her with Gems, and beautiful treasures
of Hematite, Marble and Malachite
When that was not enough I pressed myself into Coal and
Diamonds,
And for a time she took me inside her, warming me, loving me.

She whispered lovingly to me when we met in museums
and talked long hours under muted light and laser beams.
How well matched we were, locked in our embraces
as long as I kept my distance.

I left my wild side in pursuit of her, the ancient beds laid
at Stonehenge, the Pyramids, Chichén-Itzá, Hadrian's wall
I longed for her curves, transparency, and clean lines,
To be reflected lovingly as I gazed awed, into her eyes-
Unaware till too late of her fragility.

She cannot exist without me.
From slow erosion of all that holds me together inside
She gets what she needs, what makes her strong.
I am happy to be broken so she can thrive.

I have to admire her from afar and leave her be
Because, I am bereaved with any advance.
I burn for her night and day
knowing that for her to live I must die
So I crumble willingly without a fight.

My Darling; beautiful, beloved Vitrina
I give you all of me.
Shine for me, come through the fire for me
Remember me, my sacrifice.

(Stone's love for Glass)

Stone Love

When first I saw you my beloved, you stood resolute
Remote, burnished to undeniable sheen –
Experience yielded craggy character of cosmic repute.
Hewn by challenges, by Eons, stark and lean
to whetted perfection, you are my dawn and dusk.

Counterpoint to my fragile iridescence
Your depth gave death to dangerous dalliance
But birthed, for your presence craving, concupiscence
Pent up hot, molten, inside and out, on you utter reliance
till flesh, from whom, I am, without you a husk.

I waited bereft, inconsolable for your return
Ignorant of the extent of your sacrifice.
Our love flame inescapable, so I yearned
consumed, for completion and you, without artifice.
Finding you in every fiber of me, love's end poignant, brusque-

Yet I do love myself
and you remain my love, my all, my dawn, my dusk.

(Glass's lament for Stone)

My Darling, my Everything

My Darling, Falcon and Lion, my King!
You've flown into my life on soaring wing
And lit this roaring flame in my heart
That warms my cold places while sweetly tearing me apart

I yearn for you night and day, my King
You are in my prayers, dreams, and the songs I sing.
There are feelings and nuances I have never felt before now
Gripping me, leading me to let you in through all my doors.

I feel like a flower that's been waiting for rain
Closed tight against the elements - to ward off pain
And now that your quiet gentle storm is here
My petals open for you releasing love's fragrance everywhere

I am your mate and Queen Lioness
Through time we'll stand together despite any duress.
This love is blessed by God's Holy Spirit,
For we seek Him together – the greatest eternal benefit.

I've learned so much about love and faith from you my sweet King
That I would not trade each discovery for any other thing.
And, I wake to each day with hope, purpose and a smile
All because you brighten my world, all the while.

When we are old and gray with little lion cubs round our feet
We'll have loved a lifetime – savory and sweet.
There'll be stories and anecdotes – even advice to share
With all who visit us and want to know what makes us still care
My Falcon, and my King, You, are my Everything.

Section 2- **Poems of Social Issues and Honoring my Roots**

Pity is a wasted thing on strays like me

Don't look at me, just walk on by.
In this ninety-degree heat
by this side street
I need to sit,
so don't look at me, just walk on by.

Ask me no questions, or try to pry.
What of my purple cheek
and festering eye?
Ask me no questions; I won't die.

Pity is a wasted thing on strays like me.
Wish my man had told me though-
before he went and loved me so.
Why love have to be like this?
Pity is a wasted thing on strays like me.

Black men aint the only ones who play this shit.
A busted lip,
or bruised hip –
Black men just aint the only ones.

Bought some Johnson's at the corner store.
Cool on Fingers,
Smooth on skin,
Need this talc for deep within,
Yeah! Johnson's, from the corner store.

What am I going to do when daylight ends?
Hang out roun' here or on subway bench.
He might have cooled down by now.
What Ah goin' do when daylight ends?

Don't look at me, just walk on by.
Night time is sweet,
hides like a sheet.
Don't look at me, just walk on by.

Share the Dream

I believe in you
and encourage you to discover,
share in, and be proud of your heritage.
Because, despite all the put downs,
You've always managed to move forward.

I believe in you
and ask you to believe.
Share the dream.

I believe in you
although your pride has been stripped from you,
and you sometimes don't feel like going on.
When opportunity's doors are still shut in your face
while white smiles pretend to fulfill their promises
and don't.

I believe in you
and praise you because,
Out of the soil of deprivation and discouragement
you've grown Scientist's, Educationists,
Freedom Fighters –
A line of greatness, that will never be broken.

I believe in you
and am mad at you
because you have become willful victims.
Wake up and take a look around you!
Drugs and hoodlum activities hold you slaves still.
Aren't you tired of saying "Yes Massa?"

I believe in you
and urge you to speak out for our brothers
whose dignity and freedoms are being squashed in South Africa,
In worlds within and without.
The White Man keeps trying to sooth us
with his famous golden tongue.
Let's talk about it, he says
While he shoots us in the streets,
Locks up our children, and makes deals
with our oppressor behind our backs.

I believe in you,
I also plead with you –
Carry the torch.
It's been soaked in the oil of our forefather's blood,
Lit by our courage and endurance
and fanned by our frustration at injustices.

I believe in You
and ask you again to believe and
Share the Dream.

Believe in yourselves
because you are Black and Strong.
Believe that one day we will rise up
and show the oppressors that –
the only future for this world is,
to stamp out the lines of demarcation and
substitute love and understanding for
prejudice and malice.

(written 1985 before the end of Apartheid)

DRUMS

Sistah let us go down and hear de drums
Boom de de Boom de Boom de Boom
Dey playing in de park til afta dark
Boom de de Boom de Bam Bam Bam
Bring yuh man and baby too
Bim de de Boom Boom Bang Bang Bang

Come Brother man back to yuh roots
Boom de de Boom de Boom de Boom
It's in de blood: yuh can't shake dis ting
Boom de de Boom de Bam Bam Bam
Don't you see all ah we can be one
Bim de de Boom Boom Bang Bang Bang

Check out the Ebon blackness of de lead man
Boom de Shih Boom de Shoom de Shoom
Shaking him dreads and winking at June
Boom de de Boom de Bam Shih Bam
Ah few whites come to look an learn
Bim de de Boom de Bang Bang Bang
Finding out their blood got rhydim too
Boom de de Boom de Boom de Boom

Birds overhead pause to reflect
Boom de de Boom shih Boom shih Boom
Dey playing in de park 'til afta dark
Boom de de Boom de Boom Boom Boom
Dis is the human game of chance
Boom de de Boom lang Boom lang Boom
Yeh Sistah shake yuh hips and laugh
Boom de de Boom de Boom Boom Boom
Drums will get you every time
Boom Boom Bam de Bam de de Bam.

> (Inspired by a summer jam session in Prospect Park –
> Brooklyn NY)

man

I see you as the lonely child, still
in that grown up shell.
No mother, no father, no abiding city:
no truth, no lie, no right, no wrong.
A latch key in one hand.

You brought yourself to school
till you outgrew it,
and quick money fit more –
when you didn't blow it.
Fast cars, clubs, and women –
a piece in the other hand.

Lonely child begets lonely child
gangster family; how long?
How long can you hold the thread
before your fingers get burnt?

Man child can't hide no more from life –
or blame whitey any more, such a shame.
Man child, child man or is it child?

Try to play by rules and win
before you knock it, excuse it or lose it.
Brother man, how come others make it?
Fake it.

(1st published in Poetic Voices of America – Fall 1994,
Sparrowgrass Poetry Forum Inc. This poem possesses separate
copyright)

Section 3- Poems for fun and Reflection

Fair is the Moon

Fair is the Moon
upon this night,
Her trailing gown
a pleasing sight.

Her gleaming crown
peeping through the trees
Out there for each
lonely one who sees.

Many a solitary soul have gazed
upon her benevolent breast.
And found, at least for a time –
Surcease and rest.

Fair walks the Moon
across the sky.
So slowly, she trails
and hails goodbye.

C'est La Vie

C'est La Vie, my dear
Such is Life,
We win some, we lose some
and we brush off the pain by saying
C'est La Vie.

But this time
I can't say anything; I'm choking!
I can't cry, or scream, or kick.
I
can only sit here and stare…

There is a pounding in my head
like a thousand thundering bulls – trampling,
Trampling, on my soul.

And echoing on the frayed threads
of my memory, a small voice
mocks me.
Repeating in the stillness of my heart
C'est la Vie, C'est La Vie,
C'est? Vie? C'est!!!

Rhymes

Rhymes
give one the hardest time
They must be a sign
That one's mind is going blind
Or
That one is sublimely
stupid.

Splat

Pitter pat,
SPLAT!
The rat
was eaten by the cat.
And that was that.

Star

Josiah came out of the woods last May.
He said he'd be gone in search of Honey,
But that was six weeks ago to the day
And Katherine had used up all their money.

He carried a fallen star in a jar wrapped in gauze.
"It hurts to hold it," he said when asked.
People would pay to see it up close
Except for the Reverend who said "It's a hoax."

Josiah soon opened up a liquor store.
You could see the star in a jar
mounted by the exit door.
And Katherine his wife would ask sweetly, "Anything more?"

He was polishing the jar in his store one night,
And inventorying the spirits with lips pursed tight-
When the ladder he was on gave up its fight,
And toppled Josiah, Rum, Whiskey and Gin
With the Star in the Jar – What a Din!

Ned ran in from next door to help
But instead was transfixed and yelped.
A starfish it was, with blue lights- battery driven.
Josiah smiled weakly and said "That's how I made my livin."

My Mother's Feet

If you could see my mother's feet
You'd see a lifetime – full and sweet
They're big and wide, steady and strong,
Got her where she wanted before too long.

Her calluses, bunions, corns and veins
Are triumphs and sacrifices along life's lanes
Long standing shows on ankle, up leg –
Round shank and plucky calf as well.

She stood for more than most will know
On lines for food – for bread, in snow.
In times when most refuse to stand
Principle and purpose always were upper hand

Despite their seemingly tortured look
They're definitely not an open book
Years of study and gently massage
Have revealed her revered life's collage
If you could see my mother's feet
You'd see a lifetime full and sweet.

Joust of Hearts

He was her shining knight
Said he'd always be her friend
Yet he took to instant flight
When his heart began to unbend

She was his princess fair
Trusting in his gallant game
But he couldn't face the scare
of being silently called by name

She followed on his heels fast
Because he must have meant all he said
This love will definitely last
If only she could dampen dread.

He spurned her staying cry
Pressing on behind his shield – chivalry
Dooming them to the endless plight
of hearts shattered by blighting savagery.

The years keep sweeping by
Changing landscape but scenery same
And still she blindly pursues
Her Knight of un-whispered name.

A Jouster's Reply

I never asked you to so enthrone
me in your heart dear
or fix your plans on me alone
because of our affair.

You were my Princess indeed
Until under all t' was revealed
That beneath the excitement of need
Fairness is a hook and bitter mead

Aye, it was partly my fault
And yours, for mistaking my amorous speeches
I did not specify my need
Commitment, Ha! Save it for the leeches.

It is not the man's fault alone
We each rush the opening acts
Before scanning script and props and setting the tone
Then woe to whom lack is found in – brutal fact!

Inelegant flight will transpire
because of the failure to comprehend
the gist of what raises the ire
of women, who men late try to befriend.

Men cannot stay and friend remain
with a prickly one betrayed
by the silent game.
After all, each party's thoughts were always twain.

Exit becomes paramount
A lout's crown is hard for some to wear
but isn't without some clout
I must wear it, so future damsels beware!

Thus, friendship should be choreographed
into salutations and opening lines
and honest intent be clearly tagged
instead of gaming with misguided minds.

Women if you want a Prince
be clear, forceful, bold and true.
From your vision never wince
And eventually, this person will claim or be claimed by you.

Princes to be, must sow their oats
Bah! In life the product another keeps-
Two things: One cannot expect a lamb to be born from goats
and Maidens won't always sleep.

Legacy

Something lasting
should be left of our time,
But what?
Oh! Of course,
Fall Out!

Wild Birds

Wild Birds fly at night
On darkened wings soaring
To and from desolate places
My heart with them roaring
Filled with yearning, thundering might.

Wild Birds somnambulant at day
tucked under pennon in spare rare trees
Hid from view mid leafy laces.
Tamed and for a time free
While others engage in paltry pedantic play.

Wild Birds – so lonely in groups
Not of a feather, not flocking together
Wild, winged, wandering, West.
Bonded by blood, heart and hidden tethers
Till Sirocco like winds toss them East.

Wild Birds are dreamers
Not so foreign in spirit or deed,
Solo flights are done next to neighbors.
Tandem thoughts can sometimes tangent be
When circling in a party of three.

Come fly with the Wild Birds at night
Spread darkened wings and soar
To and from desolate places.
Fill to the brim your heart with roaring,
yearning, thundering might.
Take flight!

(After a night with friends at Dan Lynch's Blues Bar, NYC)

Survival

I
could not tell a lie
so I almost died.

Since then,
I was convinced.
So now I always lie
to save my hide.

Cloud Nine

Today
I realized what it was like to really walk upon a cloud.
My friend's laughter, and company,
surrounded me like wisps of floating gossamer cotton.
I was insecure and a bit timid as I am wont to be,
But today
I walked upon a cloud, And I was happy.
(17th birthday)

A Day in A Glade

Dawn crept up to the sky
like a timid child on its mother.
Its tentative fingers splayed around her midriff.

A single bird
on a single tree began to entreat her
to shake its hand.

A downy triplet
of sugar candy clouds floated by
as friendly fireface shone
and smiled through her baby blue bonnet.

An emerald field shook
and shimmered with a breeze
and the cricket ensemble disbanded
with the birth of the new day.

The streamers of heat
fought the earth for release from their bonds
and Gaia did give.

Lizards and Ants,
snails and snakes
exchanged news and gossip
on and off the job.

A Second bird
fluttered
and landed close to the first.

The last of the workers
trudged down his hill
while whispers of wind stirred the twigs, branches, leaves, and
grass,
and fireface sighed!

Two feathered friends
sang their goodbyes
as evening closed its curtain on the stage of the sky.
And a Star appeared.
(Age 15)

A Musical Wonderland

Did you ever notice
how musical animals are?
All around us they give their tribute to nature.

The insects,
small though they are,
Give beauteous sounds.
Termites at a convening, click,
click, click, click,
gossiping about each day's intake of wood.
A screeching wail and all is quiet.
The head termite has called the meeting to order.
Music! to our ears.

About a mile away, perched on a tree,
A natural born reed expert,
The Death's Head Hawk Moth,
Is piping away an exquisite melody
that rivals even human standards.

The Robin and Nightingale in a rare moment
lend their deliciously divine voices –
Soprano, Alto, to the harmony of a trio:
Two voices and a flute
harmonizing, blending, separating,
and blending again,
enjoying life,
praising the divine.

A foray of Leeches near the pond beyond the tree
begin to accompany them; tap, tap,
tap, tap, tap, tap,
tapping on the leaves,
a snare drum added to the natural trio.

Two crickets and a lone beetle
give their applause
and the trio accepts their cries of encore.
(16 yrs- inspired by Lewis Thomas' Lives of A Cell- Sounds
insects make)

Clichés

People who live in glass houses should not throw stones.
Why not? Let them, how else to find out that hurting others only
hurts yourself.
You only live once, how else will the truth, tactfully said of
course, set you free?
Throw stones from a window or balcony!
Then you can climb or jump down and run away before they return
fire.

Men seldom make passes at girls who wear glasses
and Beauty is in the eye of the beholder
unless your vision is blurred because you are older
or you are the Beast in love with Beauty
which makes the whole thing awkward when the Beast puts on his
glasses. Seriously!

But if you are a man who wears glasses
it makes sense to make passes at girls with glasses
Unless; you are counting on opposites to attract,
You see it takes two to make a thing go right
and then they will just be like two peas in a pod.

Time heals all wounds unless you are mortally wounded
from the stone thrown by the louse in the glass house.
What if you don't heal because Time took the bus home early?
You see, she waits for no man.

But I heard that Time was kidnapped by Procrastination.
At any rate you are just out of time
and luck ran out leaving you high and dry
then the only thing certain at that point is death and taxes.

If Procrastination is the thief of Time
Would he know what to do if he's running late?
I bet if they were having a conversation he 'd say to her,
"I'll get to it just wait a minute
or I'm late, I'm late for a very important date."

Would she then reply? "What's the rush? Take your time,
You are right on schedule. There is plenty of time for that
because there is always tomorrow just take one day at a time."
But Procrastination ponders as he approaches Time
"I should not put off what I can do today till tomorrow."

He hesitates still reflecting - Haste makes waste
and if we talk it over eventually Time will just stand still
then, she will be easy pickings.
Finally he says "Oh well I guess there is no time like the present.
I will have to strike while the iron is hot."

The people you meet on your way up are the same you meet on
your way down.
Who do you meet then when one door closes and another opens?
Is it the person who yells Na ah, shut the front door!
Or Mr. Opportunity who only knocks once
and maybe only at the exit, side, or back door?

Keep your friends close and your enemies closer,
I don't know about you but
I think it would be easier for them to get you, even if you see it
coming.
But then if you have frienemies-
it is indeed a moot point. It will be two for the price of one.
Keep smiling, keep shining, knowing you can always count on
them and watch yourself because a person is known by the friends
they keep.

So let's look at the whole thing from a different view point.
A bird's eye view will certainly give us perspective.
When we agree to disagree no one can take a dim view of the
other's vantage point?
Even if you are certainly, most definitely not; seeing- eye to eye.
Someone must be looking at the world through rose colored
glasses or living in la la land.

But if you choose to see it my way
we can see that Clichés are Cliché
It is easier to say pithy picture phrases that describe one's point of
view.
You get the picture right, because a picture is worth a thousand
words
and who wants to begin a journey of a thousand steps
when you can take only one.
Because it's well known that a stitch in time will certainly save
nine.
Time is happy to wrap this thing up so you all come back now ya
hear!
It was nice to meet you. No really, I insist, the pleasure was all
mine.
That will be all folks.

It aint over till the fat lady sings but this thing already had its Swan
song
There is no chariot swinging low for to carry it home.
So once again thanks for coming and Good night.

Section 4 - **Poems for those who live in Glass Houses with stones in the Closet**

The Rape

"I don't really want to do anything" he said.
"We won't" She said as she bounced on the edge of the bed
"Can we at least fool around a little, relax,
you're tripping to the max."
"Ok, but I don't want to go," he said, "all the way.
Remember, we discussed this yesterday."
Smiling she agreed. "OK.", "Are you sure, anyhow?"
"Sure," she smiled and laid her head in the crook of her arm she'd bent like a
bow.

She touched him in secret places above and below
He kissed her and stroked her, her inner spaces to know.
Soon, their breathing quickened – He felt so close.
She was delicately flushed like a pink rose.
He felt he couldn't take it anymore. Should he stop it now?
She hovered and sank on him - a ship docking at a familiar shore.
Sensation blazed – he tried to cry no and push up
but he met her arms and mouth
and his own body's weakening, and treacherous release.
She smiled, suddenly strong, and held him down while tears trickled south
"You OK?" Her gentle tones whispered.
She smiled again more triumphantly in the aftermath.

He felt queer, why didn't she or he stop before or wasn't he able to throw her off?
"What have you done?" he thought but said "Yeah sure."
She held him close yet he felt so cold.
She said, "I hope you didn't feel pressured but it was so good."
"I think," he said, "I'm hungry, do you have any food?"
While they cooked and talked about mundane things he felt strained,
out maneuvered, bereft, shocked, confused and so, so cold.
She kept searching his eyes, her eyes faintly guilty yet crowing, so bold.
He met her eyes with disbelief and fear in his.
His celibacy was now a lie since he gave in.
What about diseases and AIDS, would God forgive him for allowing this sin?
Was I raped if she took advantage when I clearly said no?
No wonder the world laughs at Christians that play with fire
expecting not to be burned when to forbidden places they go.

Not so secret embraces

I caught a glimpse of them on the way to class today
two ladies in a secret embrace, entwined to my dismay
Later on they said they were coming out
yet on one's face was a shadow of doubt
It was something each had secretly wondered about
and with new found freedom, opportunity tantamount
so they experimented and flaunted their love bravely.

Pundits say each is born with feminine and masculine
Testosterone and Estrogen one chemical off- rush like adrenalin
when the passion is up and one is in one's cups.
It is a spirit that more vice like grows once one has supped.
They said they were born that way and were drawn deeper darker
to liquid musky encounters more wild and partners berserker
still one doubted aching for freedom from this body of death.

There was a guy across campus she kept running into
he had eyes for her too but what exactly should she do?
This thing had grown a life of its own
and about campus for it she was known
How to let the other revelers know she wanted to come out
from among them and not scandal shout
or cause introspection of modus operandi and motives.

Finally she was caught in intimate embraces
and could spout no disclaiming clause when put through paces.
Campus reeled and once red lettered in sweat pants hooded
She flitted on boyfriend's arm staunchly but yet he brooded

Years have passed and happily married they care for three
One day she saw her old love in high glee
at her child's excellent dental prognosis.
At coffee while kids played they reminisced – re the progress of time
Recounting events and people mutual known – quite a long line

Old lover had remained with her lady
while others drifted off waywardly, married
It seems when asked why one had in such lifestyle tarried
and others shed skin in which they'd sworn they were born.
There was no clear answer but questions posed forlorn.

Are some really meant to be that way or lust, curiosity and rebellion driven?
We will never know but are cautioned not to judge just love.
All will be revealed when we see who'll be found in heaven.
Does tolerance mean forgetting the Creator's stance

and allowing children to consider lifestyle choices
like having corn or maple syrup on one's blintzes?
When has it ever been that because everyone is doing it,
then it must be alright and truth?
A loving God will not condemn or judge.
But then God is everywhere and found
in so many ways these days,
He, she, an idea, or even yourself, if you in meditation stay

When the created lose sight of the sovereignty of God
Challenge and make Him into our own idea of who He should be
then we create a Deity who exists on paper,
or is a puppet or amputee

He has nothing to prove but is capable of humbling
us from beyond the veil as we mill around bumbling.
Why should we stop what we want to do and curb
or cut out desires? A loving God will understand?
Really now! Just as he understands hubris
and rebellious costly choices

No wiser we drown in what we think is best,
as He lets us, till it cloys
then true obedience develops in some. Faith accepts no decoys.
You see he does have a plan for us if we accept that
God as God can do and declare as he pleases as a fact.
The pot cannot usurp the chef to plan and cook the meal,
add ingredients and execute with finesse
The artful beauty of a dish well served.

And others who swing the other way
to want to crusade, curse, cut down people without parley
remember the only judge sits in Heaven on the throne
and will not suffer those who in his name disown.

It remains - they will know we are Christians by our love
and let those who are without sin cast the first stone
Live like Jesus in relationships accepting sinners not sin
speaking truth, revealed from the Holy Spirit within.
Let His light in you, others win
True words from above.

Section 5 -Poems of Faith

Eyes Burn
(Eternity)

1.Eyes burn,
Throat Clogs,
Tears?

2. Spit blood,
Enamel falls,
Gums.

6. Live, Laugh
love God,
Eternity.

3. Breasts sag,
Developing flab
Panic!

5. Tummy Tucks,
Spend more bucks
Foolery!

4. Hair thins,
Dye and Wigs,
Old Age

Night Places

Sea of faces
Frowns and traces
of laughter,
float up through spaces
at Me – a daughter of tonight.

Expectancy laces
each brow and bases
all slaughter,
of ideals. It races and curdles
in the mortar and pestle of
avaricious insight.

Hymn of all races –
Disco enriched basses
Echo through the rafters.
Looking for love in dresses from Macy's
Navigating blind on this empty flight.

Night Places
Cannot fill our spaces
Yet with diligence some plead their cases
Only God can permeate and leaven us –
Causing us to rise,
to be transformed by his might.

When Loneliness Leads us

So, when loneliness leads us to pine
We listen to music – have some wine
Turn the lights low, maybe light candles
Sipping and swaying in the glow.
Remembering, remembering, remembering
And wishing!

So, when emptiness fills us gaping wide
Some turn to God – others keep the void
open; ever denying, walking on.
Souls dipping and swaying on celestial waves
Searching, searching, searching
and still wishing.

So, I know this God of mine can fill me
yet - it doesn't stop my beating wings
or prevent pain from earthly things.
To live close to Him I can only do,
If down on my knees I constantly go
believing.

It Amazes Me

Daily we walk life as strangers redeemed
Spreading a word of love, peace, and joy
Trying to live as examples and give reasons why
To those who ask. How can we exemplify
A God who says his Son is the only way
To Truth, to life, to hope, to eternal joy?
We cannot make you into our image
But must humbly know you as your spirit shows us
How You give, and gave, it amazes me

When I was little on my Father's knees
I got a glimpse of your majesty
In the stories from your word so true
I saw your face in the drops of rain
Falling upon the world and removing stains
Of dust and grime, - healing from pain
At just the time we need to be free.
You are there to find us if we would yield to you.
You give, and gave, it amazes me.

Chorus
For it amazes me
Just how you came and took the world from sin
Although they did not know it then and still don't know it now
You Gave, and give, and live within
If we stay under your protective bower
And accept your love and redemptive power
Yes it amazes me.

Joy!

Joy, Joy, my Savior gives
He holds my hand and walks with me
He bears me up in sympathy
He knows my cares, calms all fears
Joy, wondrous Joy!

When I first came to the Cross
I saw only Christ's sadness at me being lost.
Then Jesus opened my heart
and showed me how to let his love start.
Such love sublime, can't be robbed by time.
Joy, wondrous Joy!

Walking in him each day
Brings new treasures my way
Yes Jesus opens each heart
and shows us how to play our part
Justified by Love, atonement unmeasured trove
Joy, wondrous Joy!

If you don't know him today
Cast away doubt from life's fray
Jesus can enter your heart
forgive you, and heal you from every dart
Death no more has sting, He gives life everlasting,
Joy, wondrous Joy!

What will you be?

Everyone wants you to be a hedgehog.
If God intended us to be that way
Then where would the sponges go?
Would there be room for rocks,
Or swaying reeds, even faithful dogs?

Everyone wants you to be a prickly bush,
Or relentless hunter of prey.
If God intended us to be that way-
Then where would the shame – o' ladies hide,
Or floating lilies and clinging vines?

Everyone want you to be a stinging burr
Quick to sting and stick at will.
If God intended us to be that way,
Then there would be no need for
Will o' wisps or Panda Bears.

Everyone wants you to be a Venus Flytrap
or female Black Widow.
If God intended us to be so one-sided
Then, would there be need of lemmings-
Who'd appreciate the sacrificial Lambs?

And yes, everyone tries to make you a doormat-
An appendage, even a rubberstamp.
But God intends you to be better than these.
What will you be?

Where the Healing Water Flows

There is a quiet, tranquil place,
In the center, the vortex of the soul
Where the healing waters flow.

One can only find it after one's
walked through emotional fires
and danced through mental and physical strain.
When one's been over the edge
and then some
and clawed and crawled one's way back.

There in the middle of all the turmoil and pain
One finds the Fountain
which,
Bubbles release and whispers peace.
The waters wash over your heart and soul
smoothing and soothing.
Cleansing and freeing.

This wellspring is blessed by God.
The Fountain-
God's Love –
incarnate in Christ.
I know where the healing waters flow.

Acknowledgements

I would like to thank God first and foremost for blessing me so magnanimously and for giving me the opportunity to share my voice. The beauty and truth of His word inspires and astounds me daily.

I would also like to thank my family, friends, special people, and circumstances that walk alongside and surround me. You have given me the moments, the flashes of light which birth poems. For this, to you all, I am forever indebted.

www.ingramcontent.com/pod-product-compliance
Lightning Source LLC
Chambersburg PA
CBHW041758040426
42447CB00001B/5